Washing My Life Away

Washing My Life Away
Surviving Obsessive-Compulsive Disorder

Ruth Deane

Jessica Kingsley Publishers
London and Philadelphia

Back cover photograph by Matthew Colborn

First published in 2005
by Jessica Kingsley Publishers
116 Pentonville Road
London N1 9JB, UK
and
400 Market Street, Suite 400
Philadelphia, PA 19106, USA

www.jkp.com

Second impression 2005

Library of Congress Cataloging in Publication Data
A CIP catalog record for this book is available from the Library of Congress

British Library Cataloguing in Publication Data
A CIP catalogue record for this book is available from the British Library

ISBN-13: 978 184310 333 2
ISBN-10: 1 84310 333 8

Printed and Bound in Great Britain by
Athenaeum Press, Gateshead, Tyne and Wear

To Roger and George

x

KIRKLEES METROPOLITAN COUNCIL	
250642113	
Bertrams	02.11.07
616.852DEAN	£11.95
	CUL44084

Acknowledgements

I would like to thank, first and foremost, Sam, to whom I will be eternally grateful.

Diane, Wendy, Mike, Stuart and Hazel – thank you. At the time when I most needed support, acknowledgement, encouragement and friendship, you were there. I will never forget that.

Roger and George. My life, my rocks and my future. My ultimate achievement by far.

Note

Where permission has not been sought or it has been considered by the author to be inappropriate or impossible to do so, the names of the individuals included have been changed.

Every possible effort has been made to ensure that none of the individuals mentioned is negatively or incorrectly represented.

Contents

Preface

Obsessive-compulsive disorder (OCD) is an anxiety condition which creates worries, doubts and superstitious beliefs that become excessive and debilitating to the sufferer. It is as though the brain gets stuck on a particular thought or urge and just can't let go. OCD is a medical brain disorder that causes problems in information processing. As with all disorders of the brain, OCD can cause extreme suffering to those with the condition and the people who are close to them.

OCD is an illness affecting more than two per cent of the population; thus it is more common than severe mental illnesses such as schizophrenia or panic disorder, although it was once thought to be rare. Research by the Obsessive-Compulsive Foundation suggests that, in the United States, one in 50 adults currently has OCD,[1] and twice as many have had it at some point in their lives. Research also shows that, despite the belief that such disorders only affect people who have experienced abuse in their childhood, OCD can in fact affect anyone, and for no apparent reason. As with all mental disorders, it is almost impossible to ascertain exactly how, why or when such illnesses take effect.

---

1 Statistics taken from British National Health Service and the Obsessive-Compulsive Foundation, July 2004.

I have chosen to write about my experiences of OCD as a former sufferer. It was important to me when I developed OCD to learn that I was not alone. I hope that by sharing my knowledge, experiences and understanding of this illness with others, this book may in turn provide an insight into the illness itself and the recovery process.

CHAPTER ONE

Muck and Dirt

If asked to describe mental health problems to the ignorant, I would say this: your brain is the most complicated organ in your body, so it is bound to go wrong from time to time, just like the other organs in us that go wrong from time to time. Not a difficult concept to grasp when you think about it!

Because the brain is so vastly complicated, it can be really quite difficult to 'generalise' when it comes to the disorders that affect it. While there are obviously going to be similarities between cases, no one case is going to be exactly the same as the next, mine being no exception.

As a youngster I spent most of my time in the company of horses, rather than humans. My sister Ann and I spent as much time as we could outside. Our ideal day would be spent getting as filthy as possible and caring not one bit about it. Grooming the horses. Mucking out the horses. Feeding and riding the horses. Horses, horses, horses. They were great.

The only time during the day that either Ann or I would consider it necessary to partake of human company would be at meal times.

'Wash your hands before you sit down, girls.'

'Why?'

'Because it's hygienic.'

'Righto Mum.'

Never did it even cross my mind that hygiene was something to worry about. It just didn't. I accepted that washing my hands was the hygienic thing to do, but I definitely didn't *worry* about it. I was a normal, healthy child, living life and having fun. I was very lucky.

A typical early morning routine for me back then may perhaps appear unimportant at this stage of my story. But believe me when I say, it is significant. In order to understand the illness I developed more clearly, it is important to see that I was not always affected by the behaviours that I developed.

So, such a routine would be something along the lines of getting out of bed and throwing on yesterday's clothes, and thinking nothing of it. I would probably forget to clean my teeth, go to the loo and dash straight past the sink. Water rarely visited my skin until bath time, and that was usually only upon the instruction of my mother. I would go straight to the breakfast table, eat whatever was put in front of me. And then I would go and get on with whatever the day had in store. Most important, I would think very little about what I was doing. I wouldn't worry about it. There was nothing to worry about.

Nothing wrong with living like that. Nothing at all.

But unfortunately for my parents, I was rather a volatile child and 'did as I did', rather than ' as I should'. Or is that volatile? Perhaps it's just normal – whatever *that* is! I couldn't work out for the life of me why my mother was so insistent that I should bath every day, wash my hands before eating, and so on…and so on… Well, actually, I did really, I just didn't worry about it. I didn't even so much as think about it. So, naturally, most of the time I simply didn't do it.

A morning routine as I have just described meant nothing to me back then. But to put myself through the same routine ten years on, with OCD controlling my every waking moment? Not a chance!

CHAPTER TWO

Vomit

By the age of 18 and after leaving home, I would describe myself as being a bit of a tomboy. I lived in a shared house with two brothers, Philip, 27, and John, 19. I worked as a part-time groom and nanny for a family not far away. In my spare time I sang for a local blues band and enjoyed very much being part of the local music circuit. I was happy.

I would often come home from work to find Philip busying himself in the kitchen. He was a tall, thin, balding man with piercing blue eyes.

His welcoming greeting would usually be along the lines of, Bloody hell! What is that *revolting* smell?'

'Horses.'

'That's disgusting. Why do you have to bring your work home all over you, Ruth?'

'Fresh country smells,' I would retort, unruffled by his abruptness, perhaps breathing in the air and coughing a little at my admittedly potent odour. 'You can't beat them.'

'No? And I don't have to join them either. For crying out loud, go and have a bath…may I suggest in bleach?'

John would arrive, also covered in mud after cycling home on his mountain bike.

'All right darlin'?' he would say to me and kiss my cheek, leaving a brown smear of mud on my face.

John was completely unlike his brother in both looks and attitude. He was stocky, dark haired and cheeky. His general demeanour was very laid back and humorous.

'Err, your brother reckons I smell, John.'
John would immediately stick his middle finger up at his brother and he and I would run outside into the garden for a play fight. Just as Ann and I would have done as small children.

Philip would raise his eyebrows and begin bleaching the kitchen surfaces while pretending not to watch us having fun outside. He was OK really; he just had different priorities in life to me. Just like my parents.

An incident I think may have been significant to the onset of developing OCD happened while I was living with Philip and John. I remember it vividly.

Driving my car home from work late on a very cold winter evening, I began to feel sick. I was very hot so I opened the car window and leaned out occasionally to breathe in the air. When I arrived home I staggered to the door clutching my stomach. Phil and John were out for the evening.

Two hours later I began to vomit. Violently.

A friend of mine happened to stop by and he stayed with me during the evening. Bless him, he was a saint. He had only dropped in on the off-chance I might be at home. It would have been ten times worse had I been on my own.

I was sick throughout the night. I eventually collapsed in bed during the early hours of the morning. It was horrendous. Stabbing pains in my groin and uncontrollable stomach spasms forcing its contents into my devastated lavatory. I don't know how, but I managed to cover the best part of the bathroom, and myself, with this vile-smelling bodily fluid.

I have always had a problem with vomit, ever since I can remember. That may seem a bizarre remark, as I am sure none of us particularly enjoys the experience. Still, I have always been petrified of it: of being sick, of seeing sick, of hearing someone throw up. The full shebang. It's gross. You could say it has been a genuine phobia for me, rather than merely a dislike.

I think something significantly changed in me as a result of what was seemingly a bout of food poisoning. Damn those prepacked sandwiches. I subsequently established that the smoked salmon and cream cheese snack I had consumed during my lunch break had not been quite as fresh as the sell-by date had intimated. Unluckily for me.

The following day I was shaking, sweating and filled with a fear I couldn't explain. I have never been a good patient. The slightest sniffle and I become very over-the-top. 'Will I make it through the night, do you think?' You know: stupid comments made in order to gain sympathy. I had always *handled* illness reasonably, though. But not this time.

Maybe this unfortunate event managed to unleash some form of deep-rooted anxiety of which I hadn't been aware until then? Who knows? Maybe it was just coincidental.

It is considered by many medical professionals and those working within the care sector that there is almost always a trigger in the onset of many mental illnesses. This theory has been thoroughly researched and there is seemingly a correlation between traumatic incidents and mental health decline.

However, I do feel in my case that there was an over-exaggerated emphasis on establishing a trigger and, indeed, a reason why I became an OCD victim. In my experience it is helpful to discuss memories and experiences which you feel might be significant to any problems in life you may be experiencing. But I don't think that it is a simple matter of establishing a likely reason for a mental illness, dealing with *that*, and waiting for the illness to go away automatically. An illness such as OCD involves the learning of unnecessary behaviours. This requires an 'unlearning' process in order for the sufferer to get better.

I do believe that traumatic or harmful experiences – rape, assault, robbery, for example – can leave us mentally as well as physically scarred. However, searching for such an experience on which to blame my OCD was counter-productive in my case. Not to mention an enormous use of time.

CHAPTER THREE

Is It, or Isn't It?

By the time I reached the age of 19, I desperately longed to go back to how I had been as a child. The child who cared so freely for life. I longed for peace of mind; to live my life with the fullness I had enjoyed back then.

I hadn't really been aware of anything other than my feelings of anxiety. I knew I wasn't very happy. I knew I found it difficult to relax. I found myself worrying about things more than I used to. I also seemed to worry about things more than anyone else did. My mind was constantly awash with thoughts and doubts. But it is only with hindsight that I can see how the pattern emerged. I didn't link my developing behaviours with my emotional self. I didn't see my behaviours as being abnormal at first, as they were not profound. So at the time it felt like one minute I was perfectly normal, and the next, I was a fruitcake. OCD crept up on me without me knowing. It wasn't until I couldn't cope with day-to-day living that I even began to suggest to myself that I might have a problem.

I seemed to develop a peculiar need to clarify, more than once, many of the everyday things that I did – that we all do. For example, I started to check, at least three times, that

I had locked the front door before I went to bed. Not unusual behaviour for a woman living alone? Surely that's just being cautious?

I mean, you do have to make sure that you are safe in your own home, don't you?

You may *think* you have locked the door, but have you?

Did you *really* lock it?

Did it lock properly?

Maybe you think you have locked it, but was that actually yesterday?

Best check it again to be on the safe side.

The iron!

Did I switch it off before I left the house?

I'll go home and check.

Let's have a look.

It's off.

Is it?

I would stare at the ceiling from my bed. Thoughts invading my head.

Did I put my cigarette out?

I'll just check.

It's out.

Oh God. Did I empty the ashtray in the bin?

I'll check.

I did.

Is the bin on fire?

No.

Best put some water in just in case.

I would go to bed. Exhausted.

Did I lock the door?

Of course, an element of this behaviour is instilled within all of us. We all value our own safety and well-being and possess a natural instinct to protect the things we care about. However, if this behaviour begins to impinge on our daily functioning, it can become a major problem.

It is quite acceptable to believe that we didn't lock the door when we thought we did and to check it to reassure ourselves. How many of us have thought we left the iron on or have forgotten if we switched off the bathroom light?

But how many of us dread waking up each morning to the fearful routine that has now become part of our lives? The checking. The double checking. The triple… Every day is the same. Every day, the mere anticipation of the need to fulfil these obsessions compulsively takes control of you, dictating everything you do.

Can you imagine that? Can you actually imagine not being able to leave your house for fear that, no matter how many times you check that the door is locked, you can't quite accept it?

This doubt looms over you continuously until you are utterly exhausted.

Did I?

Didn't I?

Should I?

Shouldn't I?

Over and over again.

That is how it all started for me. The door checking and the doubting thoughts.

Then the washing began.

OCD can manifest itself in three forms. You can be a 'checker', a 'washer' or, as in my case, both. I would wash my hands. And then wonder if I had washed them properly.

I'd do it again.

And again to be sure.

Did I do it properly that time?

Did I rinse them enough?

Did I use enough soap?

I'd do it again.

My thought process was bizarre. But to me at that time, it was completely necessary. If I didn't obey my thoughts by carrying out these actions I would feel compelled to do them again and again until I either satisfied myself or was simply too worn out to carry on.

The obsessions got worse and the compulsions more intense. They also became very difficult to hide and, even more, to explain. It's easy to explain why you have double checked the door is locked. But try and explain why you feel it might be necessary to rinse your hands a certain number of times each time you wash! Not exactly average behaviour.

All I knew was that it seemed to make me feel better if I did it that way. I had a routine in my mind that had to be adhered to. If I didn't follow it then my life was not worth living. The emotional drive exceeded the fear that this might be irrational behaviour. At the same time I actually knew that this was exactly what it was: irrational. But out of my control.

I didn't know what was going on. I was 19 and becoming trapped in a lonely world all by myself. I was the only one who knew and felt these things and so I had to get on with it.

It seemed so bizarre that I didn't tell anyone about it. What was to tell? I had gone mad. People don't want to know that. They stop talking to you. They stop being your friend. They look at you differently. It was best not to tell. So I coped by myself.

What would I say anyway? 'Oh. Err, I don't know if you feel the same as me but…germs appear to be everywhere. They must be washed off all the time. You must walk up the stairs 14 times each night, mustn't you? That way you can prevent something bad from happening, can't you?' How mad would that sound?

Not only was I washing and checking to excess, but I had also developed another strange thought process and behavioural pattern.

I often told myself that if I did certain things everything would be OK. It was a bit like the treading-on-the-cracks-in-the-pavement game most of us play as children. If you don't tread on the cracks you manage to achieve something. Or alternatively treading on all the cracks might instil a feeling of satisfaction which would lift the spirits. The philosophy is the same. Whatever the physical act, the desire is to try to 'make' something good happen by wishing hard enough with the use of a tangible process to add weight to it. Most of us know that wishing alone is unlikely to 'make' something happen. So why not add a bizarre ritual to make all your dreams come true? That way it will have to work? Won't it?

Similarly then, I would convince myself that by washing my hands in a particular way, or by walking up and down the stairs a particular number of times, I would feel calmer.

I didn't though. Not really. The more ideas I came up with the less effective they became. They were simply add-ons to my obsessions and compulsions. It seemed as if life could not have got much worse.

CHAPTER FOUR

A Sink at the Altar

By the time I was 21, this strange behaviour had become a part of me. I had become accustomed to the fact that this was how life was going to be. Forever. I couldn't simply revert to my former self. I knew that if I didn't check the door, the iron or my hand washing then I would have to take responsibility for the consequences. I couldn't cope with those feelings of dread. So, for a while, I just got on with it. I had no choice.

After all, you can't just undo beliefs. Once you believe that green is green and the sky is blue, you can't just change that. Just because someone tells you that green is now blue and the sky is pink...well, it just doesn't work like that. If I didn't check the door then it would inevitably be unlocked. That was that. I couldn't take the risk.

It was around this time that I met my future husband. Nice bloke: steady, reliable, you know...nice.

During the first few months I managed to avoid any questions he asked about my slightly odd habits. I didn't ask him about his habits, so why should he ask me and expect an explanation?

I assume now that he must have noticed that I had a rather strong relationship with soap and water. Maybe he didn't? He presumably fell in love with me for *me*, OCD included, as this was very much part of my character when he met me.

At this time I didn't actually know I had OCD; I didn't even realise there was such an illness. I knew I was ill, or at least 'not quite right', but I was very much in denial of it all. I was just a weirdo.

After dating for a matter of months, we decided to get married the following July, just under a year later. A bit quick, possibly, but discussion is irrelevant because we did it.

The stress involved in organising the 'big day' nearly sent me completely around the twist. And wash! Did I wash? I did nothing but. Wash. Wash. Wash. Check. Check. Check. In fact, if I could have organised for a sink to be installed at the altar I would have done, believe you me.

This increased stress had a significant effect on the intensity of the illness. As OCD is an anxiety disorder, this stands to reason.

I have to say, though, that if it hadn't been the wedding that increased my stress levels, I'm sure it would have been something else. I don't blame this event on my decline in health but it was, at the time at least, significant. Yet I wouldn't consider it a 'reason' for becoming worse. Why? Because most people get married, but they don't all develop a mental illness as a result of it.

The wedding day itself was fantastic. All went according to plan. No hiccups, no glitches, just clockwork perfection. However, I have to confess to visiting my doctor a week or so beforehand and he prescribed a handy supply of Valium for me. I took rather a large helping on the day itself. You know, to get me through the nerves.

Did I want to spend over two hours in a situation which prevented me from washing my hands? I did not. Really, it was that bad. My own wedding day, and my most prominent thoughts were of fulfilling my obsessive needs as and when I felt compelled. With a great deal of help from the Valium however, I managed to get through the day.

The weather was fantastically hot, everyone turned up and a good time seemed to be had by all. For a split second of bride-like madness I even managed to go to the toilet and wash my hands just the once. What did I care anyway? I was completely out of it!

As I recall, for a short while after the wedding my life seemed to improve a little. I still washed and checked, but the changes I had made to my life had somehow taken up a great deal of the time I had previously devoted to OCD.

However, as it turned out, this distraction was not due to my overwhelming happiness about becoming a wife; it was merely the result of a further development of my illness.

CHAPTER FIVE

Best Before...Never!

It had become necessary for me to wash my hands frequently for the purpose of removing 'germs'. However, I had also started to think and worry about other ways in which germs could spread.

If I didn't wash my hands before preparing food I thought that I might become contaminated with something. But what if the food was contaminated before I prepared it? This was not something I could control.

When exactly my fear of contamination developed I know not, but I do know that once it took control things became much, much worse.

If milk were closer than three days to the sell-by date, I would throw it away. I stopped eating certain foods altogether. I believed chicken potentially contained salmonella, so I would not take the risk by eating it. The same went for pork and duck. Soft cheeses and yogurt were removed from the weekly shopping list, lest they contained listeria. Anything else was relatively OK, just as long as it was consumed on the same day as it was purchased and the refrigerator was at exactly the right temperature.

Phew! It was exhausting.

After we were married, my husband and I would often find ourselves spending the night in, watching television. Every evening he would try his best with me. He would predictably ask the question:

'Would you like any tea?'

'No thanks', I would always, even more predictably, decline.

'What have you eaten today?'

'I've eaten OK. Stop fussing.'

'Cup of tea then?'

'OK. But let me make it.'

I would always have to make any item of food or drink I intended to consume myself. I couldn't cope with not knowing how it had been prepared or whether or not fresh ingredients had been used. I would walk rigidly and feel anxious whenever I entered the kitchen. In order to make a simple cup of tea, I would have to go through a long-winded procedure:

Empty the kettle.

Rinse it out three times.

Fill it halfway.

Boil water.

Empty kettle.

Fill kettle again.

Boil water.

Wash hands.

Choose clean mug very carefully – check absolutely clean (impossible).

Wash mug regardless.

Add water to tea.

Check milk…

'When did you buy this milk?'

'I didn't, you bought it.'

'Did I? When?'

'Today.'

'Are you sure?'

'Yes. Don't worry. It's as fresh as a daisy.'

I would sniff the milk anyway, regardless of this reassurance from my husband. Even if a third party reassured me, I didn't believe them. I would take the tea through to him. I wouldn't drink mine, despite the palaver I had gone through to make it.

Before long, my weight had reduced to just over five stones. At five feet ten inches tall, that was not a pretty sight. Neither did I feel very well. I can't have been taking in more than 300 calories a day. My blood pressure was dangerously low and it took everything I could to summon the strength to get out of bed in the morning.

I felt sick, weak and hopeless. But I still managed to wash my hands. By then I had no option but to succumb to my obsessions; I thought that they helped me. So I just got on with it.

CHAPTER SIX

Sunday Diver

Somehow I coped with my everyday living. How I did that, I do not know. I began working for a local newspaper, which seemed to keep me going. I found life much harder to cope with at home, everything seemed to be heightened in my own environment. I don't know if it was because I had more time to think when I was there. Maybe. I wanted everything to be perfect. To be clean. I was responsible for that at home, so I went to painstaking lengths to achieve it. You could have eaten your meals off any surface in my house. Not that *I* would have done, mind you.

At work I felt I could at least switch off for a while and focus on something other than washing and checking. Also, I knew that it would have been rather bizarre by anyone's standards if I had started cleaning my desk and immediate surroundings, rather than doing my job. Having said that, I did have a handy supply of disinfectant wipes in my desk drawer. It was very hard for me, but I managed to cope.

It was a desperate struggle every morning to leave my house. But as soon as I turned the key in the ignition of my car, a temporary sense of relief would sweep over me, giving me a meagre moment of peace. In fact, driving had become a form of escapism for me. I felt alone in my car and in complete control. I often drove for miles just to escape from it all. It seemed to help to calm me down.

Days of inevitable difficulty for me would be those when someone visited my home. I could hardly wait for the visits from my mother-in-law, for example. She was a lovely lady really; she just didn't have any empathy for my weird behaviour. I put this down to her generation and their old-fashioned beliefs about mental health.

She fitted the image of a mother-in-law, if you know what I mean. Sort of overly motherly in a grey-haired, comfortable kind of way. I quite liked her and I think she liked me. But at times, and for what I can only put down to her being prey to a typical mother-and-son syndrome, we religiously and almost competitively pretended to disapprove of each other.

In anticipation of my visitor's arrival one particularly humid afternoon, I recall rushing desperately upstairs to wash my hands.

And again.

And again…

With the usual thoughts of trepidation madly filling my head I repeated the hand wash some 20 times.

Wash, wash, wash…temporary relief…wash, wash, wash.

The horrendous feat that lay before me was to prepare the Sunday roast. A simple enough task you might think? Not for me it wasn't.

I tried to give myself a stern two-minute pep talk. It seemed to help for the duration it took for me to tell myself that I was being irrational. I brushed away the hair that had become stuck to my forehead, took in a deep breath and…panicked!

For the next two and a half hours I prepared and cooked the lunch. In between each procedure of peeling the vegetables and preparing the sweet, I vigorously washed my hands. I repeated this ritual many times until it felt right, the sad fact of the matter being that it never *did* feel right.

Everything had to be just right. It had to be cleaner than clean.

Exhausted and about to drop, I heard the doorbell ring. In walked mother and son ready for their meal. I managed to exchange vague pleasantries and make my apologies before retiring to bed. I needed space for a few hours of uninterrupted panic attacks. And I certainly couldn't face eating a meal.

I ran upstairs with my arms stapled to my chest, my pulse racing and the sound of my own breath invading my head. I dived into the bathroom and washed. I was completely fatigued. I felt I had been so rude by leaving them to eat alone, but I really couldn't help it.

I lay rigidly on the bed staring up at the ceiling.

I'm truly mad.

I just wanted it to go away.

Please someone. Make it go away.

CHAPTER SEVEN

The Hypnotic World of False Memory

Life continued in this vein for months and months. Some days were better than others but, on the whole, my life was a desperate struggle. OCD had taken control of me. It determined my existence.

Of course, subsequently, my marriage was distinctly affected. My husband and I didn't bother to acknowledge each other's presence, let alone engage in civilised conversation. It had gone beyond that.

Occasionally we would mutter a word or two out of forced politeness. But it was obvious he couldn't cope with me. And frankly, neither could I.

'Hi,' he would mutter as he walked in after a day's work. Without waiting for any response from me, he would scuttle past at the speed of light. He was so obvious in his deliberate attempt to avoid any form of communication with me. It was almost funny.

He would shut the kitchen door behind him. Charming.

'Bloody hell!' I would think to myself. 'I must be a complete freak. He won't even talk to me now. Maybe it's me? Maybe it's him? Yep. It's him. He's stupid. That's it. Stupid. He's stupid. Perhaps I'm stupid? Yep. We are the stupids! I'll simply stop this stupidity and it will all be over.'

Off I went to wash my hands.

The time came when I finally held up my hands, pardon the pun, and begged for help.

I don't know if it was then that I admitted fully to myself that I had a problem; or that I was just so stressed out that I felt I needed someone else to take a view on my situation. I made enquiries into just about every form of professional help available, from counselling to herbal remedies. I searched the Internet and my local library. Eventually I decided on hypnotherapy.

My little knowledge of this procedure was only really based on television programmes such as *The Hypnotic World of Paul McKenna*. I simplified it all I think, out of pure exhaustion and desperation. I decided that the idea of going to sleep and waking up better was more than appealing. So I told my husband that this was what I was going to do.

Perhaps I relayed my simplification mechanism to him because his immediate response was that he felt an hour or so with a hypnotherapist would be sufficient to revert me to normality. Whatever that was. It was this response that made me feel that he actually had no understanding of my illness, or me, at all. This more than irritated me, but at the same time it came as no great surprise.

I began to believe that if it were as simple as my husband believed it to be then it wouldn't work. It couldn't possibly. Coupled with what I considered to be ignorance on my husband's part and my own belief that I would never recover anyway, my scepticism overwhelmed me. I became angry and shouted at him.

'Some weirdo bloke telling me to "sleeeep" is not, I repeat, not, going to make a scrap of difference! I mean if it were that easy I would be better surely? I do go sleep every night, don't I? One visit and I'll be better…how can you even think that? I'm not going.'

We got into the car.

He said nothing to me during the journey. He parked the car, got out and led me to the door. I was very nervous, but intrigued all the same. It had to be worth a try.

The door opened and a strange-looking gentleman greeted us. He looked like a vicar to me. We were obviously at the wrong house. I tugged at my husband's coat in a bid to leave. But…it was him. This was the hypnotherapist.

I stared at him curiously, I'm sure he must have noticed. I decided I didn't like him, or rather, I wasn't going to like him. He was weird. And definitely not a vicar.

The three of us sat down in a very dark room on an equally dark sofa. The wallpaper was yellow and beige and the ceiling a rather grim shade of nicotine brown. And as for the carpet stains, they seemed to get bigger the more I looked at them.

The horror I felt at sitting in such a vile and disgusting environment was about as much as I could take. Needless to say, the cup of tea I was offered was instantly refused. If that was the state of the sitting room, then I had no intention of sampling the hygiene level of his kitchen.

After a mind-numbingly boring and long-winded intro-duction to the marvels of hypnotherapy, the weird bloke and I left the room and retired to the treatment area. I took the stance of a grumpy teenager and dragged my feet as I walked. I refused to speak and just followed his instructions. I reluctantly lay down on the couch, making absolutely sure that he was more than aware that I was totally unimpressed with the 'wonders' he professed to be able to achieve.

He didn't seem to sense my deliberate attempts to provoke him. He just asked me a few questions, which I answered minimally and very sarcastically. I actually enjoyed behaving so badly. I found him dull and boring and disbelieved everything he said.

Due to the boredom, I managed to turn the experience into a game within minutes of arriving. Or did I do so out of nervousness? Anyway, I found it irresistible to pull childish faces at him every time he turned his head away from me. I avoided any form of eye contact with the poor man and almost began to pity him for the way in which I was treating him.

He was getting paid though.

He seemed oblivious to what I considered to be obvious complacency and carried on regardless. I had by then become convinced that he was a robot and had been programmed to answer specific questions. I even tried giving him an answer to a question he didn't ask, to test my theory. But even that didn't raise a glimmer of interest. His nasal tones of voice and speech impediment didn't help either. My boredom enhanced the need to eject an uncontrollable fit of the giggles, which did nothing for my concentration.

Eventually I must have drifted off. Apparently the hypnosis lasted for about an hour, although it seemed much shorter to me.

I was so desperate at that time that I felt that if there were something real or tangible to latch onto as a reason why I had become so troubled, then this would help me to recover. At that time I was so alone, isolated and confused. What I really wanted was to speak to, meet or read of someone else who had whatever it was I had. That would make it tangible. I think that maybe I had thought that the hypnotherapy might be able to reveal something 'real' that may have happened to me to cause the illness.

But the hypnotherapy session revealed nothing other than a few vague possibilities, none of which I could single out as being a true reason for my becoming ill.

I didn't feel that the experience was beneficial to me at all. But what it did do was put to bed some of my desperation to find something to blame. I had now come to the realisation that even if there was something that had caused this to happen to me, it didn't really make any difference.

This was the way I was. I didn't like it; I wanted to get out of it and now I accepted that I needed help – and I intended to get it.

CHAPTER EIGHT

Basic Concern

I visited my GP on a more than regular basis at this time. I was convinced that every slight ache or pain was the onset of a serious illness. I suppose I would actually have preferred that then: at least I could have had something wrong with me that I understood, and that other people understood. Whatever was wrong with me was weird and seemingly unexplainable.

My GP suggested that I should visit a counsellor and as I agreed he made a referral immediately. I felt that he would have done anything to reduce the number of visits I was making to the surgery. I'm sure he did care that I was obviously not well, but he didn't seem to understand me – or at least, that's how it felt.

On my first visit I told the counsellor that I had been to see a hypnotherapist who had made various suggestions about my past. With hindsight, I felt that the experience had been quite traumatic for me and I had received little sympathy from my husband.

The hypnotherapist had made intimations during the procedure that maybe I had suffered at the hands of someone as a child in an inappropriate manner. I had no recollection of any such happenings and felt disgusted by the mere suggestion. I knew that it was believed by some that the mind is capable of hiding painful or traumatic events and experiences. I also knew that there were many therapists operating throughout the world who believed that this is the root cause of much mental health decline.

It seems that this theory is based on opinion rather than evidence. After all, it is so very difficult to prove. But at the time I could see the appeal of it. If there was something, anything, of which I wasn't consciously aware that was the root cause of my problems, then maybe, by finding out about it, I could recover. How fantastic would that be?

But, indeed, how *dangerous* could that be? Particularly if it were not true. Imagine visiting a therapist who, after whatever form of treatment, told you that you had been abused in some way. But you have no memory of it. Imagine how that would affect you, and your relationships with friends and family.

Also shocked by what had happened, the counsellor talked it all though with me. She said that if I had no memories of the suggestions made by the hypnotherapist then they were very unlikely to be true.

She did feel that it was possible that the hypnotherapist had not been a genuine practitioner and had made an assumed diagnosis based on the limited information I had given him. She stressed how important it was that any help I was offered should be directed through my doctor and not self-sourced.

I continued to visit the counsellor for a few weeks. We talked and talked about many of my worries, which seemed to help. Sadly for me, she had no real experience of OCD, which defeated the object a little. She was there to listen.

But I needed help to get out of the hell hole I was in: talking just wasn't enough for me.

When I told my husband that I wasn't going to see her any more he instantly presumed that I was better. Typical. He asked me if I had learned anything from the counselling and whether or not I now knew why I had developed the need I had for washing so much.

Washing so much. How terribly simple. Is that all he thought it was to me? Just washing a bit more than average? His curiosity, his desire for there to be a reason for my problems, simply confirmed to me that my feeling was right. The answer to when and why I had developed OCD was not necessarily the route to recovery.

I had often thought maybe I had become obsessive because my parents had separated during my childhood, or because of the food-poisoning episode. But, as I pondered the matter and explored my memory, I found several possible triggers. It became more and more clear to me that I could never determine which of these factors, if any, were responsible. In addition, it was impossible to determine exactly when it had started, thus complicating further any attempt to pinpoint the reason for it. OCD can affect anyone at any time and for no particular reason.

I managed to console myself by believing that perhaps if my perceptions were as simple as my husband's then I wouldn't have become ill in the first place. I decided he was basic. Bless him. I longed to see my life in black and white; I wished away the analytical confusion that I had a tendency to swamp myself in; I wished I was him.

Funnily enough, however, this basic conversation between my husband and me prompted me to take a good look at my life and where I wanted to be. I knew then that I could no longer be married to this man. He was everything many women would dream a husband should be but, unfortunately, not for me.

My realisation gave me an enormous emotional lift. But it also made me feel sad and guilty and, worst of all, that I had failed. For a marriage to break down at any stage, let alone by the time you are in your early twenties, seemed appalling to me.

How could I tell my husband? How could I tell the family? Was it really worth hurting so many people just because I felt that I was probably with the wrong man? After all, a marriage is not something you can just walk away from. Somehow I would have to find the courage to do what I felt was for the best: not just for me, but for both of us.

I spent weeks deliberating my next move. The pressure almost drove me to suicide. The situation I was in made me feel trapped and distressed. But the thought of what I felt I needed to do in order to move forward filled me with an even greater horror. It seemed my only escape would be some form of slow, painful self-destruction.

My panic attacks were at their peak of severity. I was constantly swallowing tranquillisers and sleeping pills. I virtually stopped eating altogether. I really didn't have any weight left to lose, but the pounds just kept dropping off. Whatever life was left within me seemed to drain away, taking me with it.

No one seemed to notice – or, at least, that was what I thought. I had become self-contained in my own world. I didn't let anyone in, least of all my husband. It wasn't that people didn't notice or care; I just wouldn't let them help me. I felt angry with myself for becoming ill. I was so frustrated because it was something over which I had no control. I couldn't casually snap my fingers and pull myself out of it. The answer was so simple: all I had to do was stop it. Stop washing, stop checking. But I couldn't, I just couldn't.

I'd had enough of people telling me to 'Stop washing your hands,' or 'Eat it, it won't hurt you.' Didn't they think I knew that? Of course I did. I just couldn't do it.

I had investigated my theories so much in my mind. Everything and anything that could hurt me, once there in my mind, had to be taken seriously. I couldn't just get rid of these thoughts. They were controlling me.

I thought that maybe if someone told me frequently enough that I had nothing to worry about it might all go away. In reality, however, that would mean having someone with me 24 hours a day, consistently devoting his or her time to my need for constant reassurance – not a job I would wish on my worst enemy! Indeed, this would have merely maintained the illness, rather than helping to combat it.

At the time, my husband's continued lack of concern upset me. It drove a further wedge between us. I think eventually he just gave up and craved normality. I could hardly blame him; it must have been a nightmare for him too. I constantly nagged at him to wash his hands and begged him not to eat the foods I was so afraid of. I felt guilty having to reject and hurt him so often. He did do his best. I remember once when he wrapped my sore, cracked and bleeding hands in a warm damp towel. He could see what I was doing to myself, but he was powerless to do anything about it. The illness was hurting him too. I could see it in his eyes.

Some members of my family also seemed to adopt the 'ignore it and it will go away' approach. Looking back, I can see how difficult it was for them too. It was hardly their fault that they had no experience of mental health problems. I wouldn't have wished it on them either. But at the time I resented their lack of compassion and under-standing. I could never work out why, when I became ill with appendicitis for example, I received an abundance of cards, gifts and telephone calls. But once armed with the knowledge that I had a mental health disorder, most of them chose to avoid me.

Part of me believed that the only reason I received such a huge response after my appendicitis was the relief that my family felt in me having something physically wrong with me, rather than mentally. They could identify with that. It was tangible. Real. They could see it. Well...the scar anyway.

A typical scenario would be when the family ate out on a Sunday. This type of gathering always brought home to me just how alone I was in my suffering. My panic attacks were always worse when I was in a social setting. Particularly when food was involved. I would sit limply, glumly staring at my plate. Waves of panic would sweep over me. Despite their intensity, no one else could see what was happening to me. Most of them just thought I was being rude and ignorant, but I was actually concentrating as hard as I could on not being sick or passing out at the table. It's quite diffi-cult to be sociable when dealing with such a problem.

A panic attack is real. It's frightening, it's lonely, it's cap-tivating and it hurts. Imagine feeling violently sick and experiencing massive heart palpitations. A significant loss of breath. The shakes. Extreme perspiration and the feeling of having a burning temperature. Imagine it and then think about feeling like that most of the time. Day in. Day out.

An attack can last anything from a few seconds to hours on end, days even. Sometimes the physical symptoms can be so frightening and severe that it is impossible to distinguish whether it is actually a panic attack you are experiencing or you are, in fact, physically ill.

I lost count of the times I was accused of making it up or attention seeking, even by my GP. But I wasn't. It was real and I hated it. I would have given anything not to feel the way I did. Anything.

CHAPTER NINE

Psychiatric Department

During yet another visit to my GP, I collapsed in the surgery. I had had enough. I was 23 and I was exhausted. Within minutes my doctor was talking about admitting me to hospital. He made a telephone call and told me that he might have found someone who could help me.

It seemed that my doctor knew personally a specialist in anxiety disorders. So it may have been due more to luck than judgement that I was then to pursue this line of treatment.

At this point my faith in the medical profession was limited. No one seemed to know what was wrong with me. The presumption was universal. They all assumed that I was 'troubled', whatever that meant, and had an over-sensitive reaction to everyday hurdles. It didn't seem that they believed that I was as ill as I felt. No one at that point had actually confirmed that what I was suffering from was OCD. I had done my own research and everything led me to believe that this was the illness from which I was suffering. Yet, because an independent medical professional had not given me a formal diagnosis, I could not be completely sure.

My biggest problem was my own denial. And confusion. Because I didn't know what OCD was, a great deal of my symptoms escaped my conscious as being relevant. For ages I didn't actually seem to know that I *was* excessively washing. Or that I *was* obsessively checking sell-by dates and the like. So when I visited my GP, I didn't really give him the full picture. If I knew then what I know now, I could have presented him with a detailed list of the symptoms relating to OCD and he would have undoubtedly told me what I was suffering from. But my emphasis was primarily on the feelings I had, rather than my behaviours. I spoke of my emotional pain, my panic attacks and my fears. But not so much of my rituals. So it was no great surprise that my doctor didn't present me with a full diagnosis.

My doctor told me that he had made an appointment for me to see a behavioural psychotherapist. This meant nothing to me. I was confused at the use of the word 'behaviour'. It implied to me that maybe he thought I was simply 'badly behaved'. I felt insulted. However, despite my confusion I was desperate to try anything that might help, so I agreed to go.

I arrived at the hospital an hour early that same afternoon. Typical of me. Always late when it matters and early when I don't need to be. I should have known that the appointment would be delayed. So I had an even longer wait.

There I sat, in a brightly decorated room labelled 'Psychiatric Department'. This was intimidating, to say the least. The more I looked at the sign on the wall, the bigger it seemed to get.

I felt dreadfully uncomfortable and began to think that everyone was looking at me and wondering what kind of mental problem I had. I made a point of trying to look confident and smile at other people and thus attempted to convince myself that they would believe I was waiting for someone else, rather than for an appointment. What I was actually doing was precisely what I was accusing them of: scanning the room, subtly trying to identify what was wrong with whom. I convinced myself that I was fine and everyone else was mad. It made me feel better, I think.

I had worked for a few years as a community health care assistant, but I was consumed so much by my state at the time that I had lost sight of, or at least put to the back of my mind, my own knowledge of mental health. I had, for goodness sake, nursed many psychiatric patients myself with a view to progressing to a career in social work. Sadly, my vomit phobia got the better of me and I had to give it up. But at this point in my illness and the level of denial I had imposed on myself, I seemed unable to resort to any knowledge I had of just about anything. It was as if I had become someone else completely and I simply didn't have the confidence to refer to my own internal bank of information. I didn't trust myself. I didn't trust anyone else either.

The hour-long wait seemed like months. On more than four occasions I left the room and decided that it was all a complete waste of time and then, in desperation, turned back and sat down again.

Suddenly, a young girl walked in and announced my name.

'Ruth, please.'

No! My cover had been blown. I stood up slowly and walked uncomfortably towards her, my eyes glued to the floor and my back bowed over as if I were an old woman. It felt like an admission of failure. Being seen by other people in a psychiatric hospital, waiting to see a doctor: I can't tell you how much that bothered me.

'Hi!' said the girl.

I looked at her briefly and thought she couldn't possibly be the doctor: she wasn't old enough. She was. Well, the behavioural therapist anyway. The person I had come to see.

Rummaging through her notes she came across my records. Were they really that large? Surely I hadn't encountered the medical profession that many times? How could they possibly justify using that amount of paper on me?

In fact, I had been in and out of my GP's surgery many times since developing this illness – probably twice a week at least. It had taken two years for me to reach this referral. So was it any wonder my records were so enormous?

'So. How can I help you?' she asked.

'I thought that was what *you* were here to tell *me*,' I replied rudely. I shifted nervously from side to side in my chair, once again convinced that no one could possibly help me.

'I see,' she said, not at all perturbed by my attitude. 'Well, your GP seems to think you have OCD and that's where I come in. I'm a therapist who has been specifically trained to help people with this illness. So perhaps you could start by telling me how you feel?'

'I feel crap,' I blurted out whilst waving my hands frantically and uncontrollably around. 'I can't stop washing myself and as far as I am concerned the whole world is full of germs and everyone thinks I'm making it up.'

The therapist, Sam, sat opposite me and nodded sympathetically. Her acknowledgement alarmed me. It seemed as if I was getting the recognition I had been searching for. But now I had it, what did that mean?

Still calm, Sam went on to ask me how often I was washing myself.

'About eighty times a day. My hands that is. I shower about four times.' I kept looking behind me to check that she wasn't talking to someone else. I couldn't believe that I had finally found someone who understood.

Unfazed by my shocking confession Sam replied, 'I see. And why do you do that?'

'Because if I don't I will make myself ill and that will make me panic. So I do it until I've done it properly.'

She remained unfazed, nodding and smiling in all the right places.

'Can you make me better?' I asked in a manner reminiscent of my husband – and I had accused *him* of being 'basic'. I cringed in recognition of my own hypocrisy.

'If you help me, I'll help you,' she replied. 'Do you want to get better?'

I burst into tears. 'Yes,' I sobbed. 'Of course I do.' I put my hands out in front of her and said, 'Look at my hands, they are so red and sore, they can't take it any more and neither can I.'

Sam described OCD as being a form of learned behaviour. Just as you learn to walk and talk, somewhere along the way you may learn that if you perform a simple action, such as washing or checking, when your mind tells you to do so, the unpleasant feelings you may be experiencing will go away. But by responding to these thoughts and fears by performing these actions, you are allowing the behaviour to continue, thus reinforcing it and making it much worse. It becomes a vicious circle, which desperately needs to be broken. To break it, a programme of behavioural psycho-therapy can be put into place.

There is no 'magic pill' and Sam left me under no illusion that it would be easy. But now I could see a way out and it felt good. I was ill and I wasn't alone. The recognition and acceptance of that was my first real step on the road to recovery.

CHAPTER TEN

Admitting Myself

For the most part life was much improved over the following few months. I was less uptight now I knew that I was finally receiving the help I needed. Quite obviously this positive change in my behaviour had a beneficial effect on my marriage and relationships in general.

However, I still knew that despite this period of remission, the deep-rooted problems in my marriage were very much a reality. We were definitely behaving in a more civilised manner toward one another, but it wasn't enough.

Day-to-day life seemed to take over for a while. Work. The house. The dog. I was still washing excessively and my panic attacks were about the same. But I did feel happier in myself.

I visited Sam once a week. It was quite a trek for me, at least a two-hour drive. The only hospital that employed this type of therapist was eighty miles away from my home. This meant taking time off work in order to maintain the continuity of the programme. I was aware that I wouldn't be able to keep it up indefinitely and that sooner or later my job or the hospital visits would have to go. It became a case of putting a price on my health or earning a wage.

What a dilemma! My health or my career? Obviously, without my health my career would be pointless, so a decision had to be made. I had only been in my job for a matter of months at that time and knew that my rights were limited. I began to feel guilty for letting down my colleagues and employer, and that in itself had a significantly debilitating effect on me.

I became seriously ill again. My frequent washing increased along with the panic attacks. I was finding life so difficult that I became exhausted with it and I was on the verge of giving up. I didn't eat. I couldn't smile. I spoke only when I was spoken to. More than anything, it was obvious to everyone that there was something very wrong with me.

My weight plummeted to less than five stone. I had now passed the stage where my illness could be handled at home. I knew this, but I couldn't bring myself to do anything about it. This would have meant admitting defeat, which is not something that comes easily to me.

I decided to inform my boss of my intentions. Arriving promptly at the office on a hot Thursday morning I felt so weak that I stumbled over to my desk and almost fell into my chair. I sat motionless, staring at the wall.

Sam had almost begged me the day before to admit myself to hospital. She was clearly worried about me and I realised that now was the time I had to do something to help myself.

The wall in front of me became blurred as my eyes filled with tears. And while the sounds of my colleagues around me faded, I felt as though I just wanted to go to sleep and wake up when it was all over.

After a few encouraging words from my colleague Hazel, I decided to do it. I have a lot to thank Hazel for. She was a very kind person who, despite not knowing exactly what was wrong with me because I didn't tell her, gave me words of hope that ultimately helped me take a step in my life which was to be my salvation.

So I did it. I rang Sam and asked her to arrange a bed for me at the hospital. I explained to my boss that I had to be admitted for tests and that I wasn't sure how long it would take. He didn't know I had OCD and I had no intention of telling him. He was the owner of a small publishing business and, quite rightly, his priorities lay with the running of his newspaper. His main concern was for his sales ledger and its diminishing total while I disappeared into the ether for some unknown length of time. He made me feel dreadful for taking sick leave, but I had to do it. So I left.

I knew as I closed the office door behind me that I wouldn't be back. So did he. I imagined as I left that he was already thinking about putting an advertisement in his paper for my replacement.

Driving home I began to feel faint and extremely drained. I had telephoned my husband to let him know what I was doing. He did offer to take me to the hospital but as I was adamant that I drove myself there, he accepted that and left me to it. Really I was in no fit state to drive, but I convinced myself and everyone else that I was. The drive took much longer than normal and, as I arrived at the hospital, I began to panic.

'What am I doing?' I whimpered to myself. 'I am admitting myself to a *psychiatric department.*' Reality dawned on me and I was scared. Despite my own knowledge of the ways in which hospitals are run, my thoughts were by no means rational. I began visualising mad axe murderers attacking me in the middle of the night. I even began thinking that I might be put into a strait-jacket on arrival.

The immense grey building loomed before me. Despite the fact that I had visited it so frequently over the past few months, it now looked different. It was no longer the welcoming place I had grown to depend on. Now it was dark, cold and uninviting, despite the scorching August weather.

I drove in the entrance to the hospital car park and immediately out of the exit. I had no idea where I was going but it certainly was not into hospital.

I drove for miles staring through blurring, tear-filled eyes. My panic intensified and my breaths shortened. Eventually I had a vague moment of rationality. I stopped the car and tried to pull myself together. With short, harsh breaths I reached for my mobile phone and called my friend Mark.

Mark had become a friend earlier that year. I had worked with him for a brief period and we had formed a strong relationship of mutual understanding. We both had difficulties in our personal lives and found it a great comfort to talk to one another and offer each other support. Mark was fully aware of my illness and had often taken me to the hospital appointments when I had been too weak to take myself. My husband had taken me once but didn't feel it was necessary to accompany me every week. So, Mark stepped in to offer the support I so frequently needed.

After my call Mark got into his car and drove to Leicester to meet me. He had known that I was going into hospital but had no idea that I intended to drive there myself. He certainly would have insisted on taking me had he known – which is probably why I didn't tell him. I had to have my car with me you see. It gave me the escape route I felt I had to have.

Mark was highly sceptical about my going into hospital. Despite his concern and acceptance of my illness, he was not at all comfortable with 'psychiatric institutions' as he labelled them. He believed that they were purely for 'mad people'. Which I suppose was rather sweet of him – not to label me as being 'mad'. He didn't see hospital as a solution. I think really he was just uncomfortable with the unknown, as I had been when I first visited Sam.

When Mark arrived we met in a local park and walked slowly together while he listened to me. He managed to calm me down a bit.

'You don't have to do anything you don't want to do,' he said softly.

As simple as that may sound, I needed to hear it. I needed to know that I was doing this to help myself and not because I was being forced to do it. His reassurance guided me back on to the path I needed to take.

I went to the hospital.

CHAPTER ELEVEN

Crisp White Sheets

When I woke up the next day I quickly realised where I was and sat bolt upright in bed.

My hospital room was full of the August sunshine and the crisp white bed linen was calming to my initial fears. There was nothing more comforting to me than a clean environment. White was a colour I associated with being clean, and here I seemed to be surrounded by it.

I could hear the other patients and staff busying themselves in the corridor. Now all I had to do was get out of bed and try out the hospital breakfast. I had been instructed that I was not to stay in bed unless I felt I needed to. I was to remain as active as possible and use the time to regain my strength by eating regular meals.

After a long and unnerving walk down the corridor I found the bathroom. I gasped and took a step back in horror. Oh my God! *A bath!*

There was absolutely no way I was prepared to have a bath. I didn't *do* baths. I had to have a shower. A bath meant sitting in a place where others had recently sat: people I didn't know; people with germs I didn't know. I knew the bath would have been clean. But to me, germs were something that hung around to spite me, regardless.

I ran back to my room clutching my towel and toilet bag. I had no idea what to do. There was a sink in my room so I began a long and painstakingly slow procedure of washing and dressing myself.

Two hours later, Sam arrived to see me.

'Good morning,' she announced brightly as she entered the room.

'For you maybe,' I retorted.

'I see.' Sam paused for a while, but was unruffled by my response. 'Is there something wrong?'

'Wrong! I can't do this, Sam. It's my worst nightmare. There isn't a shower. The patients are all mad and I'm scared. No one seems to have the faintest idea what OCD is. I mean – what kind of place is this?'

I was shouting and managed to take all my frustrations out on the one person who was able to help me. But it didn't feel like that to me. Not then.

For the first time since we met, Sam actually seemed angry with me.

'I'm just doing my job, Ruth. If you don't think that I have your best interests at heart then you might as well go home.'

Blimey. Not the response I had expected.

I stood staring out of the window feeling stunned and confused. But ultimately her tactic had achieved the desired response.

'Sorry,' I said, 'I didn't mean to take it out on you. But you do understand how frightened I am, don't you? I really don't know if I can do this.'

I could see from her face that Sam did understand – completely. We talked for a further hour until I became more relaxed and prepared to give things a try.

What to do with the rest of the day was left for me to decide. I felt extremely weak although I had not yet worked up an appetite. So I went for a walk through the hospital grounds. Alone and able to think I found it therapeutic to walk in the sunshine and not worry about what time it was or where I should be at that moment. Time was my own and I liked it.

Sam put me on a programme to help me redefine my behaviours. It was explained to me that in order to get better I needed to learn how to revert to my former self. Just as I had taught myself OCD behaviours, such as washing my hands an incomprehensible number of times, I was now to learn that I didn't have to. I was not being blamed for my illness or accused of learning to do these things deliberately. But by curbing my behaviours I would begin to recover and regain a sense of control. I needed to be able to see that what I was doing didn't actually have to be done to function safely in the world.

This was not the first time Sam had tried to implement such a programme of help, but I had constantly refused to do it. It frightened me too much. Once in the hospital, however, I had 24-hour support from people who could help me: I didn't have to do it 'alone'. I knew it made sense but when I actually saw the programme…I was petrified.

Here is a list of the requirements I was given for my first two days:

Ruth's tasks for Thursday and Friday

- To wear one set of underwear on Thursday and one on Friday.
  (I had developed a need to change my clothes and underwear up to ten times a day.)

- To sleep with the same bed sheets on both days.

- To wear the same night-dress on both nights.

- To drink three hot drinks per day.

- To eat two slices of bread for breakfast and a meal at lunch time.

- To keep a food diary and fluid intake chart.

On the bottom of the list was a notice, which read:

Notice to staff: Please take a food tray into Ruth's room at meal times and clarify her food intake.

Notice to Ruth: Write down what you think you can try to do as part of your programme.

As simple as that routine may sound, I had immense difficulty in sticking to it. I did manage to drink three drinks and eat a meal; as for the rest of it – no chance. And this was despite the fact that I had voluntarily admitted myself to hospital and decided that I needed and wanted help. In fact, when initially presented with my list of tasks, I became very difficult and obstructive. I knew I was behaving badly, but the fear was too great.

Didn't they understand, these people? I couldn't eat like they could. I couldn't be like them and do these things. I couldn't complete the most basic, everyday functions.

Strangely, at the same time that I knew I couldn't do it I also felt that, if I were brave enough and attempted it, then I might actually be able to. Then again, there was that fear, that inexplicable fear that prevented me from trying.

Every time I ate or drank anything thoughts invaded my head. I would vividly imagine the process by which it had been made. Who had made it? What were they like? Were they clean? Had they washed their hands before they made it? Did they have a contagious illness? Was the milk fresh? Was the water boiled properly?

Every mouthful I took, every sip I swallowed, was like drinking poison. I was utterly convinced that it would harm me, it would ultimately make me sick – that was my biggest fear.

After consuming any food or drink I would pace the corridors of the hospital for ages and attempt to convince myself that I would be OK. I would ask anyone and everyone if I was going to be OK.

'That cup of tea. It was OK, wasn't it?'

'The toast I just ate, it *was* fresh bread they used, wasn't it?'

At home I had always badgered my husband about everything I ate and drank. Was it OK? *Was* it? He would constantly reassure me, but it was never good enough. I would never be convinced and I would still panic. In the hospital they refused to reassure me. The programme of therapy didn't permit that. It was explained that I had to learn for myself that drinking and eating were normal and essential parts of life. Of course I knew that. I wasn't blind to my behaviour: I knew it was irrational, but I could do nothing about it.

The problem for me though was that there was no guarantee that the food and drink *wouldn't* make me ill. There is always a risk of contamination. I didn't want to hear that, yet that's what the staff told me. It was, of course, fact. But I wanted to know that *nothing* would *ever* hurt me – I didn't want so much as a glimmer of risk. However, that was the process I had to go through to get better.

Anyone with OCD who is to be cured must risk facing their fears. They need to be exposed to whatever it is that they are avoiding. For me it was potential contamination. For others it could be the feelings of dread they experience if they don't carry out their rituals properly, or the right number of times. Nine times out of ten there is always going to be a risk for an OCD sufferer. A logical one. For me, it was the risk of transmitting germs into me through some external source which ultimately would make me sick. This, of course, is possible in everyday life: there are germs everywhere, and every so often we come into contact with them and become ill. With OCD in control those germs become magnified. Not that I thought I could see them or anything, I had no hallucinations; but my mind was obsessed by the potential risk.

At the mere suggestion of facing my fears I would panic. Once it was explained to me that this was the process I would have to go through to recover, I fully understood it. I could see the logic. But I was too frightened to attempt it for a very long time. I would say it must have taken me 18 months in all to finally agree to so much as attempt it.

Eventually I reached the point when I had to take the risk and work through the anxiety. It made me feel stupid. I felt like an outcast. A reprobate. A person like no other. I didn't fit into anything. I was a lonely person and only I understood myself.

I felt that everyone looked at me as if I were different. That they were all talking about me and how weird I was: my family, my friends, the people in the hospital and even people on the street. I felt that they could see inside me. But they only saw that I wasn't trying. They believed that I could 'pull myself together' if I wanted to. I thought they believed that I was deliberately maintaining my illness.

But I knew I wasn't. How I wished, longed, would have died for the ability to 'pull myself together'! But just as I knew how I felt, I didn't know. My state of mind predisposed me to self-doubt, which is a fundamental part of OCD.

I could also see how strange I must have been to other people. The whole concept of OCD was so odd while the answer seemed so simple: just *stop* it and start again. It isn't that simple; it is terrifying. The doubts I felt that others had about my sincerity in wanting to recover affected the way I perceived myself and confused me all the more.

I felt torn. I knew that this was the help I needed and I understood that the way to get better was by relearning my behaviours and facing the fears I so desperately dreaded. Knowing and doing, however, are worlds apart.

I began thinking that maybe I should just accept myself with OCD and just get on with my life the way it was. So what if I washed my hands? So what if I changed my clothes several times a day? So bloody what! I wasn't hurting anyone. I could be doing many things that were stranger or more dangerous, surely? I wasn't seeing that it was dangerous to *me*, it was hurting *me*, and the people close to me. My thinking was just another way of escaping my fears. I had to face them and I can't tell you how frightened I was by that. Even if I so much as thought about attempttng to face things I reached a place in my mind where everything went blank. I wouldn't even allow my thoughts to visit my fears.

In the hospital, to start with, I think I did everything I could to challenge the staff by testing just how much I could get away with. Despite my understanding of my illness and the route to recovery, I did nothing to deal with OCD.

So I changed my bed sheets every day. The staff on the ward lacked much knowledge of OCD, so I was able to change my bed seven times in one day. I convinced the staff that the sheets I continued to get from the store-room didn't fit my bed. The same sheets fitted every other bed in the hospital, but not mine! Oh, so plausible – I think not.

I actually couldn't understand why they didn't seem to think it was strange that I kept walking up and down the corridor with sheets in my hands. Time and time again I walked past them with a stupid false smile on my face. I was laughing to myself at how easy it was to do. I failed to see that I wasn't hurting anyone but myself by being so awkward.

I continued changing my clothes as often as I liked. I did everything I knew I shouldn't be doing. The staff just let me get on with it. Bizarre. My obsessive thoughts were driving my compelling actions exactly as before.

Mind you, when Sam found out she was not pleased.

It may seem that I was foolish to have told her that the staff didn't seem to be participating because she was bound to react. Yet, although I felt happier conforming to my irrational thoughts and feared facing my fears, I also wanted to get better. I could see that I needed everyone's involvement even to begin to achieve my goals. Sam gave the hospital staff a full briefing on OCD, and this enabled them to act effectively within the therapy programme.

I was the only person to have been admitted with OCD to that particular hospital that year. While OCD is most definitely more common than you might think, it is quite rare for a sufferer to become so debilitated with it that hospital treatment is the only answer. This was, of course, one of the reasons why the staff were so unfamiliar with the disorder.

Now, despite my bloody-minded attitude, I wasn't going to get away with it any longer. It was game over for me and another reality check was needed.

Sam gave me that!

I went over the things I could and couldn't do with Sam and we devised a programme together. The following list of tasks may appear strange but, at the time, to attempt every single one of them filled me with an overwhelming feeling of anxiety.

Weekly tasks

- Shower in 15 minutes, Monday, Wednesday and Friday only.
- Wash hair on Tuesday and Thursday.
- Wear same set of clothes for two days.
- Wear one set of 'germ clothes' during the week. (These were clothes that I was afraid of wearing as I associated them with illness, i.e. I had worn them when I had been sick at some stage.)

- Wear 'germ' jewellery every day.

- Change bedding on a Sunday night and use the same bedding all week.

- Wear same night-dress for three nights.

- Use a towel twice.

- Put 'germ clothes' in wardrobe with clean clothes.

Daily tasks

- After smoking a cigarette do not wash hands.

- Use telephone and do not wash hands for one hour.

- Touch all toilet door handles on the ward and do not wash hands for one hour.

Food

- Eat a prepacked sandwich from canteen.
  (This is what had caused the vomiting episode when I was 19.)

- Eat a bag of flavoured crisps.
  (I had become convinced that any crisps other than plain ones would make me sick.)

- Eat yogurt.

- Eat three meals a day.

- Drink three hot drinks a day.

- Keep fluid and food chart daily.

I also managed to keep a diary when I was in hospital. This is what I wrote on two occasions:

Wednesday 8th August

I had a row with Sam today. She calmed me down though, bless her. I want to get better so much. I have agreed to give the treatment a go. I'm more scared about this that I am about anything. I hope someone, somewhere, is watching over me.

Tuesday 13th August

I've had a bad few days and I haven't even had the energy to write my diary. Yesterday I wore jewellery I have avoided for over a year. I also wore clothes that I haven't worn for ages. I even ate a prepacked sandwich and a packet of crisps. It was all too much for me. I feel useless. These are ordinary, everyday tasks that everyone except me can do. I have panicked all afternoon. I can't face this. I feel terrible unless I am clean. I can't do it.

CHAPTER TWELVE

Humble Pie

One evening after dinner – which I hasten to add I hardly touched, despite the nauseating, obviously pre-scripted, encouraging remarks from the staff on duty – I visited the smoking-room. It was quite crowded and I was forced to sit next to someone. I hated that, I liked space around me, but I had no choice.

I took the unsociable approach and lit my cigarette while staring straight ahead.

The man next to me smiled as I sat down. I didn't acknowledge him in any way. I thought he looked OK, but being as he was in a hospital for mad people, he clearly wasn't.

A few minutes later he asked me for a light. I hesitated for a moment and then struck a match for him so as to avoid any contact between us. I hated touching people or objects which had been touched by other people. Or indeed, any other objects. When I opened a door I always covered my hands with my sleeve and I did the same when I switched on a light or someone shook my hand. Obviously there was a limit to avoiding having to touch things but, when I could, I would.

The man asked me exactly what I had dreaded from the moment I had walked into the room. He was very direct and it took my by surprise.

'Are you a washer or a checker?' he said.

Ooh er!

Overwhelmed by his obvious knowledge of my illness I had no choice but to answer him.

'How do you know that I am either?' I replied nervously.

'Forgive my presumptions, but I know Sam, the girl who looks after you. I know what she does because my best friend had OCD and she was here last year.'

I was actually relieved that someone in the hospital understood what was wrong with me, albeit a patient rather than a medical professional. I also felt extremely exposed and paranoid that this man had assessed me prior to even introducing himself. Having said that, this was exactly what I had been doing with every single person in there myself.

'She's better now, if that's any help,' he said.

'What! You mean completely better?' I asked incredulously, as if it were a total impossibility.

'She has a trace of it, but not enough for you to notice,' he said and then changed the subject entirely. 'I have schizophrenia by the way.'

Ooh er…again!

My mouth dropped to the floor and I was utterly baffled as to what to say to him. He seemed so intelligent, so normal. I felt ashamed of myself and asked him how long he had been ill.

'For about three years. I was in my last year at university, sitting my finals, and all of a sudden Adolf Hitler spoke to me through the walls of the room I was sitting in.'

Ooh, ooh er!

'It was the most frightening experience of my life. But there was nothing I could do about it.'

He had been so open about it, almost blasé. It shocked me tremendously. I began to feel guilty and rather cross with myself. For the past few days I had been wallowing in a world of self-pity, criticising all those around me with serious mental health problems, including those I actually knew quite a bit about. The social pressure and ignorance I had experienced as a sufferer had clearly got to me in a major way. I had become a victim of what I had once fought against: I had begun to assume that to be mentally ill you also had to be unintelligent. I had convinced myself that I was sane and everyone else was barking mad. How wrong I had been! I cringed at my ignorance and decided there and then to stop being a rude, ungrateful individual and face up to myself. I was going to get better.

This is what I wrote in my diary that evening:

> Being a patient in a psychiatric hospital has made me feel so many different ways. Mark and Dad both think that this is the wrong place for me 'amongst mad people'. But we are real people in here and we are simply ill. Not mad. Why am I saying this? I already know all of this. We are in pain. Now I feel guilty for allowing myself to be taken in by social ignorance. Please someone help me to get better.

CHAPTER THIRTEEN

Living Again

It seemed that a positive turnaround in my attitude was crucial to my recovery. I would say that this was largely due to two things: Prozac, and a belief in my psychotherapist and the treatment I was getting.

So is drug-taking the answer? There are many conflicting views about this, but in my mind it is simple. If by taking medication the pros outweigh the cons, then it must be worth a try. It is not a failing to require medication to help you feel better. We take aspirin if we have a headache, and there is no difference between taking aspirin and taking Prozac other than the ailment itself.

As a result of the combination of medication and therapy I began attempting and ultimately achieving my goals. I came to the conclusion that if I didn't even try I would never know if I could achieve anything or not. It couldn't get any worse, so it was definitely worth a go. I believe that it was the medication that gave me the emotional boost to attempt the therapy. Therefore, the combination of medication and therapy formed the route to my recovery. It was a slow process but the more I achieved the more motivated I became. It was empowering. Bizarre, maybe, that managing to go through more than a few hours wearing the same clothes or eating three meals a day could possibly be described as 'empowering', but to me it was, at that time, a monumental achievement. Not only did I feel proud of myself, I began to have a clearer understanding of the behavioural therapy objectives. The more I understood, the more I could see how difficult life would be for me if I relapsed into my old ways. This gave me hope and yet more motivation to continue and succeed.

One of my biggest fears arose from my scepticism. I believed that the treatment I was receiving might help me in the short term, but I couldn't believe that I might ever get to a stage where I could confidently feel that I would never again get as ill as I was then.

After reaching a level both Sam and I were happy with, I was able to leave the hospital. I continued to see Sam on a regular basis and stuck stringently to my behavioural therapy plan. With a great deal of time, effort and courage, my life began slowly to return to normal.

I tackled my tasks, despite the pain it put me through. I accepted that it wasn't going to be easy and gritted my teeth and got on with it. There was no easy answer, no escape. I had to help myself: in effect, it was *me* that was in control.

How did I feel when I attempted a task? It's so hard to explain. I would mentally prepare myself. I would clear my mind as best I could and the longer I managed to resist the feelings of angst flooding my head, the easier it became. I had to *ride through* the unpleasant feelings I experienced when a thought pushed at my mind.

I did use some breathing exercises to help with this. One of the best and most successful breathing exercises I learnt, was not simply to breath deeply until I felt better, but to actually *hold* my breath.

I found it very difficult to lie back and relax while imagining tropical beaches and waves crashing against the sand. You know, the usual epiphany of relaxation. Time and time again Sam had tried to get me to do that. I can see that for some people it evidently does work; not for me. It actually annoyed me. Sitting still has never relaxed me. When I told Sam how difficult I found this she suggested that, whenever I felt the onset of a feeling of panic, I should hold my breath for ten seconds, then breathe out slowly and follow this with a few deep breaths. This apparently slows the heart rate down and in turn reduces the hyperventilation often brought on by a panic attack.

I had always assumed that hyperventilating was when someone obviously breathes excessively, quickly and noisily. Sam explained that some of the most powerful panic attacks were silent and apparent to no one other than the sufferer. That was what mine were like. I tried to disguise them out of fear that people might smother me, or think I was weird. I preferred to be on my own when I had an attack. The last thing I wanted was for people to fuss over me telling me to breathe.

Hyperventilation restricts the airway, which becomes narrow and tightened, creating an inability to catch your breath. By slowing the process down the airway begins to open and breathing becomes easier. The faster you breathe and the shorter your breaths, the less oxygen your body receives. Therefore, not only is breathing difficult but you can feel very light-headed and ill as a result.

These feelings reminded me powerfully of being ill, so a panic attack soon became confused with a physical illness such as a stomach bug. If I felt the slightest bit light-headed I assumed I was going to be sick; I became convinced that I had food poisoning or that I had somehow contracted a gastric illness. On that assumption my attack would go into overdrive and it would become almost impossible to get out of it.

Some people find that blowing into a paper bag helps them in the same way that holding my breath helped me. I also found that taking exercise reduced the symptoms of a panic attack. A quick brisk walk or run really seemed to calm me down.

What, in fact, was the worst thing that could happen? That was what I asked myself. A simple concept, maybe, but it was hugely significant to me. I remember my very good friend Diane saying that to me one day when I was at a particularly low point. Just one sentence, one thought, but one that most definitely helped me get better.

The longer I managed to resist the desire to give in to myself, the stronger I became. It wasn't easy though. The feelings of dread, fear and loneliness were desperately uncomfortable. The more I resisted, however, the more I began to accept that nothing was actually going to happen, despite my fear that it would, and the more I began to accept the irrationally of it all and see a light at the end of the tunnel.

I think that it is important to know that there are many different forms of treatment available for anxiety disorders. Different breathing exercises, ways in which to release tension and feelings of anxiety. A good psychotherapist should be able to determine what will best suit the individual sufferer. Sadly, there are some therapists who are quite rigid in their beliefs and attempt to indoctrinate their patients with processes *they* feel are best, irrespective of their suitability to the person requiring them. Since no one case is going to be exactly the same as the next, surely they will not require exactly the same treatment? So, if something didn't work for me, I tried something else. There is nothing more frustrating then attempting something you are advised will help you and finding it has no effect whatsoever. But that doesn't necessarily mean that there isn't something out there that will help.

The same applies to medication. There are many different medications available to assist with the symptoms of anxiety. There are some that are hugely beneficial to one person, and useless for another.

Amongst the medication I was prescribed was *Prozac* (fluoxitine), an antidepressant often used in the treatment of OCD. The usual dose given for depression is 20 mg. At the height of my experience of OCD I took 60 mg per day, which was gradually reduced to 40 mg per day. This dose was particularly effective for me. At 20 mg I found no benefits from taking the drug.

Other antidepressants I tried were *Seroxat* and *Imipromine*. Neither of these seemed to help me. This is not to say that they wouldn't suitable for someone else.

I was also prescribed *Diazepam* or *Valium* – this can be prescribed for short periods of extreme anxiety. As it is a highly addictive drug it is rarely prescribed on a long-term basis. It has an immediate sedative effect. I was occasionally prescribed this when my panic attacks completely prevented me from eating and drinking.

During the time I had spent in hospital with little to do but consider myself, I made some life-changing decisions about my future. I left my husband and started a new life on my own. Despite this being something I had always feared, I braved it, determined that life had something more to offer. If I could achieve the tasks presented to me in the hospital, I could do anything. I constantly believed in myself and that my future would be content without the pain I had known for so long.

My husband and I were not happy together. Our marriage had taken place at a time in my life when it shouldn't have done. There was nothing wrong with him – he did his very best. We just were not compatible. It was sad, but with hindsight I know that the decision to part was definitely best for both of us.

It took about another year for me to reach a level of life that I could feel comfortable with. I asked for very little – merely a life without dominant anxiety, a calmer life with unexaggerated fears. A life I could control and feel happy with.

I think that one of the things I learned during my hospital stay was that I had far too much time on my hands. I needed a focus. Something to look forward to, aspire to and get my teeth into. I think we all need something.

So I decided to set up my own business, a small publishing company which set about producing magazines for the armed forces. I had learned through my therapy that if you took a chance with something you could in fact gain from it. I had taken a chance with my illness: the chance that, if I tried to face my fears, I might get better. The chance was paying off for me so taking another one was not so hard to do. I had worked for other people who had set up in business. They had done it, so why couldn't I? I took that chance. And I have never looked back.

I wouldn't like to say whether or not setting up my company helped me to progress with the recovery of OCD. It could, of course, have hindered me as it did take up an enormous amount of my time – time that could have been spent concentrating on completing my tasks. On the other hand, it may have been that as a result of this new work I didn't have as much time on my hands to worry about obsessing any more; it could equally have been that it was my confidence and motivation that was allowing me to achieve both my recovery and my ambition for my company.

Within a year of my setting up the business it would have been apparent to no one that, just months previously, I had been in turmoil. In fact, I was so much better that, if I had suggested to any of my colleagues that I suffered from an anxiety disorder, they would certainly have thought I was joking. Ruth? Anxious? Hardly! Are you mad?

I was confident, bubbly and full of life. My whole demeanour was sparky, but amusing and laid back. And I felt this way too. I had my life back – I was living again.

I have no doubt that there will be some people who know me who will have no idea that I was *ever* a victim of OCD. But that in itself should surely be a testament to the strength of my recovery. I managed not only to reach a level of life I was happy with, but virtually to eliminate the disorder to the point where no one can detect its past within me.

I thought I was always going to have OCD. I thought there was no possible way I could rid myself of the behaviours and thoughts that controlled me. But I did. And I am proud of myself for it. It makes me believe that if I want something badly enough, I can have it. If I work hard enough, if I want it enough, it can be mine.

To be so ill, so low and so much in pain and then to climb out of it is a feeling that can only be experienced, not explained. It is pure relief. Pure heaven.

CHAPTER FOURTEEN

Onwards and Upwards

Getting over OCD was a task far greater than any other I have achieved. When I was ill my priority was my illness and my thought processes were invariably negative. My priority in life now is to 'live it' and 'love it'. My thoughts are now more positive than not. But perhaps I would not have the ability to believe what I do now had I not experienced life at its lowest point. Such an illness can offer a person the insight and ability to prioritise and take nothing for granted. I believe I am a better person for it.

To this day I still wash my hands a little more than is considered 'average', but it is to a manageable degree and does not prevent me from doing all the things I used to avoid.

Why do I still wash my hands? I think it's just a part of me now. There remains a chink in my character that I believe stems from the OCD. I understand it now and have the experience of knowing that it is not the end. It can get better: there is life after OCD. That's the difference between me then and now. Then I didn't see an end, I couldn't envisage life without OCD.

If ever I catch myself washing a little more than perhaps I should, I deal with it there and then. I will always remember how bad it was and *never* do I want to go back there again. I am stern with myself and no matter how compelling the urge may be, I plug myself straight back into my 'task list', the fear of which I no longer feel because I understand it too well. I see the irrationality of the fear and I know that you can get over it.

I say to myself, 'Ruth! You are not that person any more. You know that you don't have to live like that again. So what a waste of time it would be revisiting a place you didn't want to visit in the first place!'

Now that might sound like a simple thing to say: does it really work? Yes, for me it does. My experience gave me true understanding. It is the knowledge and acceptance of it that led me to my recovery and subsequently the ability to remain where I now am.

Of course there are still times when I feel low and times when I feel anxious. I consider myself to be of an anxious disposition: some of us are. I have experienced numerous stressful events in my life, as have we all, and the association of those feelings remind me instantly of when I had OCD. I think that the fear of returning to that place is one reason that stops me from relapsing, but the strongest form of restraint I feel that I have is *knowledge*.

The information I gained through psychotherapy and about the process of OCD itself has created what I can only describe as an explanation in my brain. When I first became ill I had no such explanation. What restricted my recovery the most was my lack of understanding. I didn't know what was wrong with me. It took the medical profession two years to give me a formal diagnosis. They had called it an 'anxiety disorder' and a 'nervous problem', but never once did they call it 'OCD'. Once I knew that it was something specific and that I wasn't alone in having it, I felt as though a massive weight had been lifted from me. That, to me, made it tangible. It was no longer 'something or other' that was wrong with me, it was an *actual* something. It had a name, it had a definition and it wasn't just me.

As with any illness it can be the 'not knowing' that is more destructive and stressful than the actual diagnosis. Of course, there are times when there is no specific answer or diagnosis, but 'wishy washy' vague guesses can be very disheartening.

I had so often simply assumed that I must have been a hypochondriac – not that hypochondria should be dismissed as being something not worthy of treatment or empathy. Had I been diagnosed with hypochondria, I am sure I would have felt exactly the same: at least I would have known *what* it was that I had. That was very important to me.

So if I ever get the urge to revert to my former obsessive behaviour, or feel more anxious than I would like, I hold my breath and give myself that very explanation. I try to remember that time in my life from start to finish, but as quickly as possible. I try not to dwell on the pain I underwent, but on the process of recovery and the end result. I focus heavily and remind myself of the end bit! Attempting the tasks and achieving them. The high I felt when I realised that this was an illness I was suffering from and that all the things that frightened me, needn't.

Once I also knew that I wasn't doing these things 'on purpose', that too helped me. When I understood that this was a real condition, and one I wasn't alone in suffering from, I could see that it wasn't my doing. It wasn't *my fault*. For ages I thought that perhaps I was making myself behave like this, that maybe I was doing it for attention, despite the fact that I hated it and would have done anything not to have been like that. It is so confusing being trapped in a state where you know that what you are doing is irrational, but you can't change it.

I make sure that, at the slightest glimmer of OCD reappearing, I face whatever I fear immediately. If, for example, I have a twinge of doubt before I eat something, a fear that it might harm me, I force myself to eat it. Obviously, I haven't gone excessively in the opposite direction! I don't force myself to eat raw chicken, or milk that's turned into cheese, or anything like that. But I try to nip in the bud any thoughts reminiscent of those I had with the OCD there and then, before they get the chance to multiply.

I also have the ability now to treat things with humour. When I am in the company of people who knew me when I was ill I can say things like: 'Oh no, germs. Get them away from me.' And then laugh. In a way that helps me; it proves to me that I can cope now and it kind of lets other people know that I'm over it too. I could never have done that back then.

When I was ill I remember going to see *As Good As It Gets* at the cinema. The film stars Jack Nicholson, whose character has OCD. It horrified me. I was so angry. The whole film seemed to make light-hearted humour out of the illness that was controlling my life. It wasn't funny. How dare someone trivialise something that was so painful and debilitating and turn it into a film?

Now I can watch that film and laugh too. I still have twangs of empathy for the suffering it caused me and that it is inevitably causing so many people right now. But the fact that I don't get angry any more is additional confirmation to me that I am over it.

I know that there is no magic pill and no fairy god-mother who can wave a wand and make everything OK. With an illness such as OCD it is our very selves that have the power to make us better. That takes strength and courage, but it can be done. Knowing that it is possible makes any task presented an easier one to face.

Something else that helps me is accepting that not everyone will understand OCD. There will be friends and family who just can't empathise with something they have no concept of. Once I accepted that, no, not everyone did understand, not everyone believed it was real, it helped me to move on. It's hard when someone close to you doesn't seem to 'get it'. But I have to ask myself if I would really want them to. After all, if they truly understood then that may be because they too have suffered in some way. Maybe not with OCD specifically, but with some form of emotional torment. So even now, when I'm faced with a lack of understanding, I try to convert the feelings of disappointment I initially have with positive ones for the benefit of whoever doesn't understand. I think to myself, 'lucky them'. They haven't felt pain like this: that can only be a good thing.

The more the years pass, the less I experience so much as a glimmer of OCD.

I am happily married now – second time lucky and all that. I have a four-year-old son and three step-children. Our wedding day was everything it should have been, and with past experiences behind me I was able to fully devour every moment. My only compelling desire was to marry the man I loved and enjoy every minute of the day I said 'I do.'

I remember Sam asking me, in an early therapy session, how I used to be before OCD took control. She said that if I could define that state of mind, and return to it, that would be my ultimate goal. At the time I couldn't bring myself to tell her. I knew if I exposed that, then she would have a full knowledge of just how much my behaviours had changed as a result of the OCD.

Despite myself, I did return to that place. I've come full circle. Roger, George and I live in a fabulous house. I *live* in our home. I don't simply exist within it. *And* I have horses again too, and I never worry about getting covered in muck and dirt when I am with them. I am just as I was when I was a child. I have achieved that goal.

Yet I believe I experience my life's loves now with even more passion than I did then. I have the experience of knowing that nothing can be taken for granted. I savour everything I love and I live a normal, happy family life.

And my business? I sold my publishing company over four years ago when I had my son. I have since spent some time studying and I am now a practising psychotherapist and counsellor. I have achieved what I consider to be many goals in both my personal life and career. Things that I could only have dreamt of when I was stuck in partnership with OCD.

I truly didn't believe at the height of my illness that I would ever see life in any other way than through the eyes of OCD. But I do, I have. And so can anyone...

Organizations

USA and Canada

Center for Cognitive-Behavioral Psychotherapy
Dr. Steven Phillipson
137 East 36th Street, Suite #4
New York, NY 10016
Tel: (+1)212 686 6886
Fax: (+1)212 686 0943
Email: ocdzone@ocdonline.com
Website: www.ocdonline.com

National Institute of Mental Health (NIMH)
Office of Communications
6001 Executive Boulevard, Room 8184, MSC 9663
Bethesda, MD 20892-9663
Tel: (+1)301 443 4513 (local); (+1)866 615 6464 (toll free); (+1)301 443 8431 (TTY)
Fax: (+1)301 443 4279
Email: nimhinfo@nih.gov
Website: www.nimh.nih.gov

Obsessive-Compulsive Foundation, Inc.
676 State Street
New Haven, CT 06511
Tel: (+1)203 401 2070
Fax: (+1)203 401 2076
Email: info@ocfoundation.org
Website: www.ocfoundation.org

The Ontario Obsessive Compulsive Disorder Network
PO Box 151
Markham, ON L3P 3J7
Tel: (+1)905 472 0494
Fax: (+1)905 472 4473
Email: oocdn@interhop.net

Australia and New Zealand

Anxiety Treatment Australia
Floor 1
140–142 Barkers Road
Hawthorn 3122
Victoria
Tel: (+61)3 9819 3671
Email: catherine@socialanxietyassist.com.au
Website: www.anxietyaustralia.com.au

OCD Support Group
PO Box 13 167
Christchurch
New Zealand
Email: info@ocd.org.nz
Website: www.ocd.org.nz

United Kingdom

Mind (registered charity)
PO Box 277
Manchester M60 3XN
Tel: (+44)845 766 0163
Email: info@mind.org.uk
Website: www.mind.org.uk

OCD Action (registered charity)
Aberdeen Centre
22–24 Highbury Grove
London N5 2EA
Tel: (+44)20 7226 4000
Email: info@ocdaction.org.uk
Website: www.ocdaction.org.uk

OCD-UK (registered charity)
PO Box 8115
Nottingham NG7 1GU
Tel: (+44)870 126 9506
Email: admin@ocduk.org
Web: www.ocduk.org